Creative Design Patterns
coloring book

This book belongs to

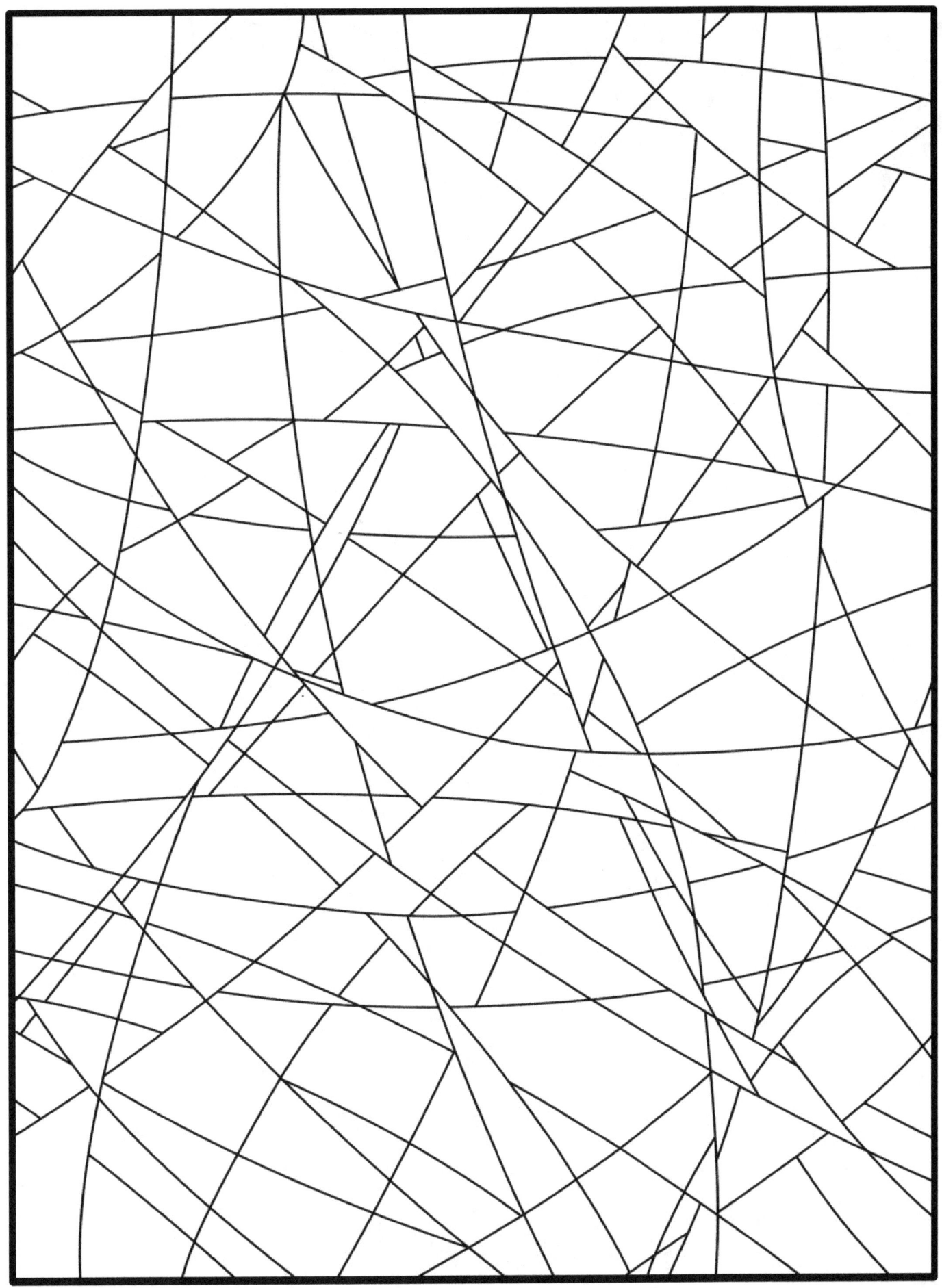

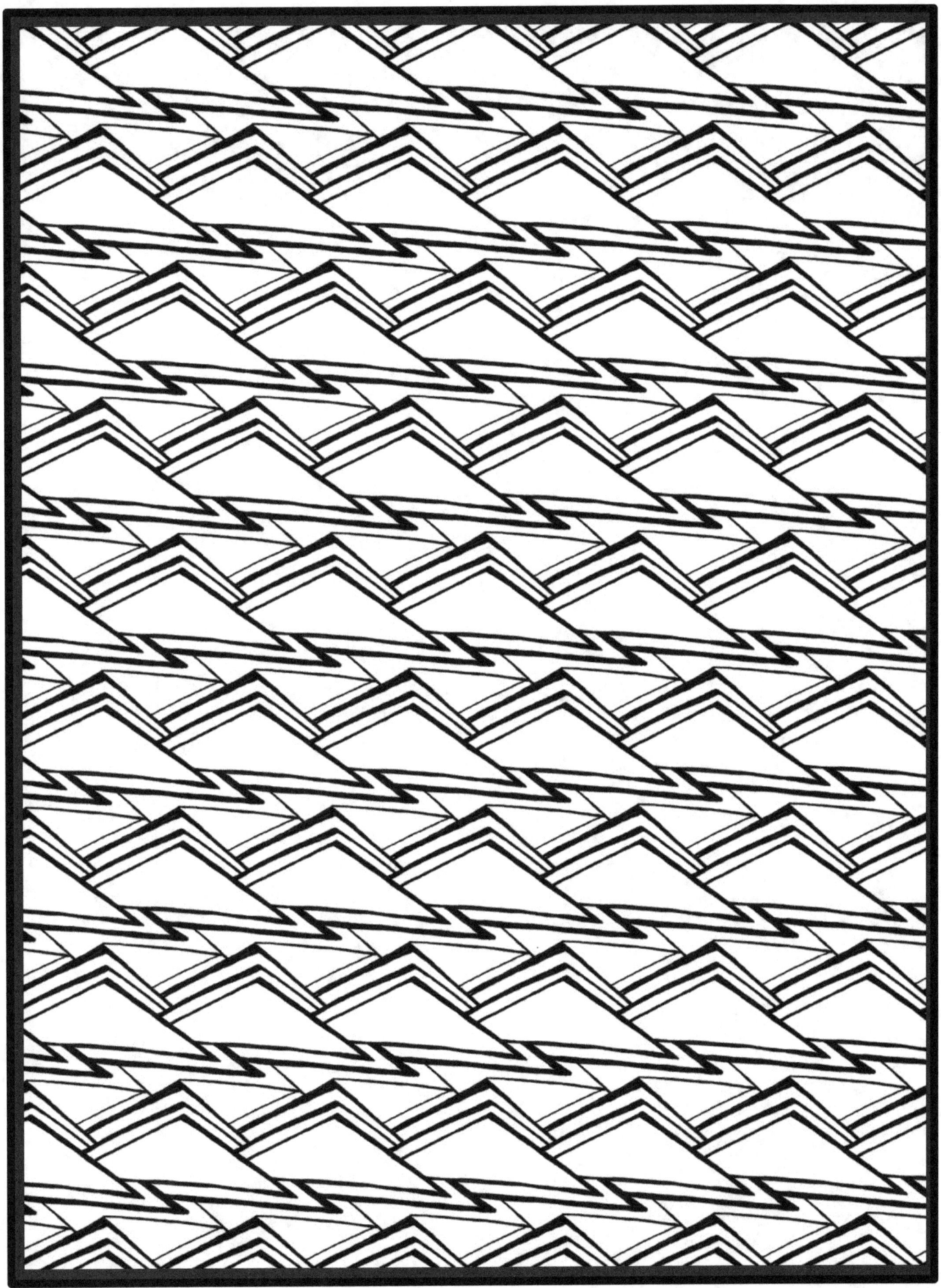

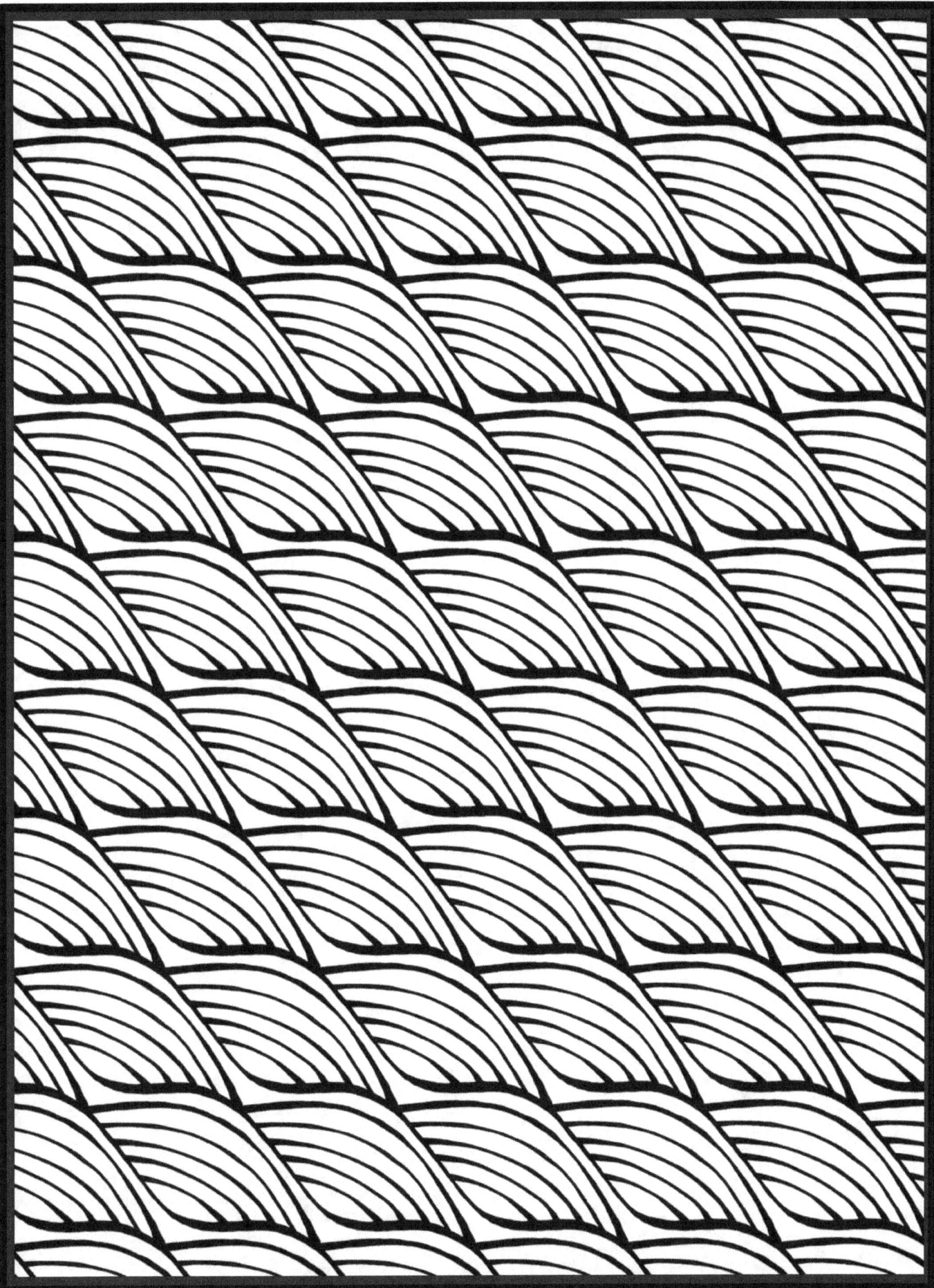

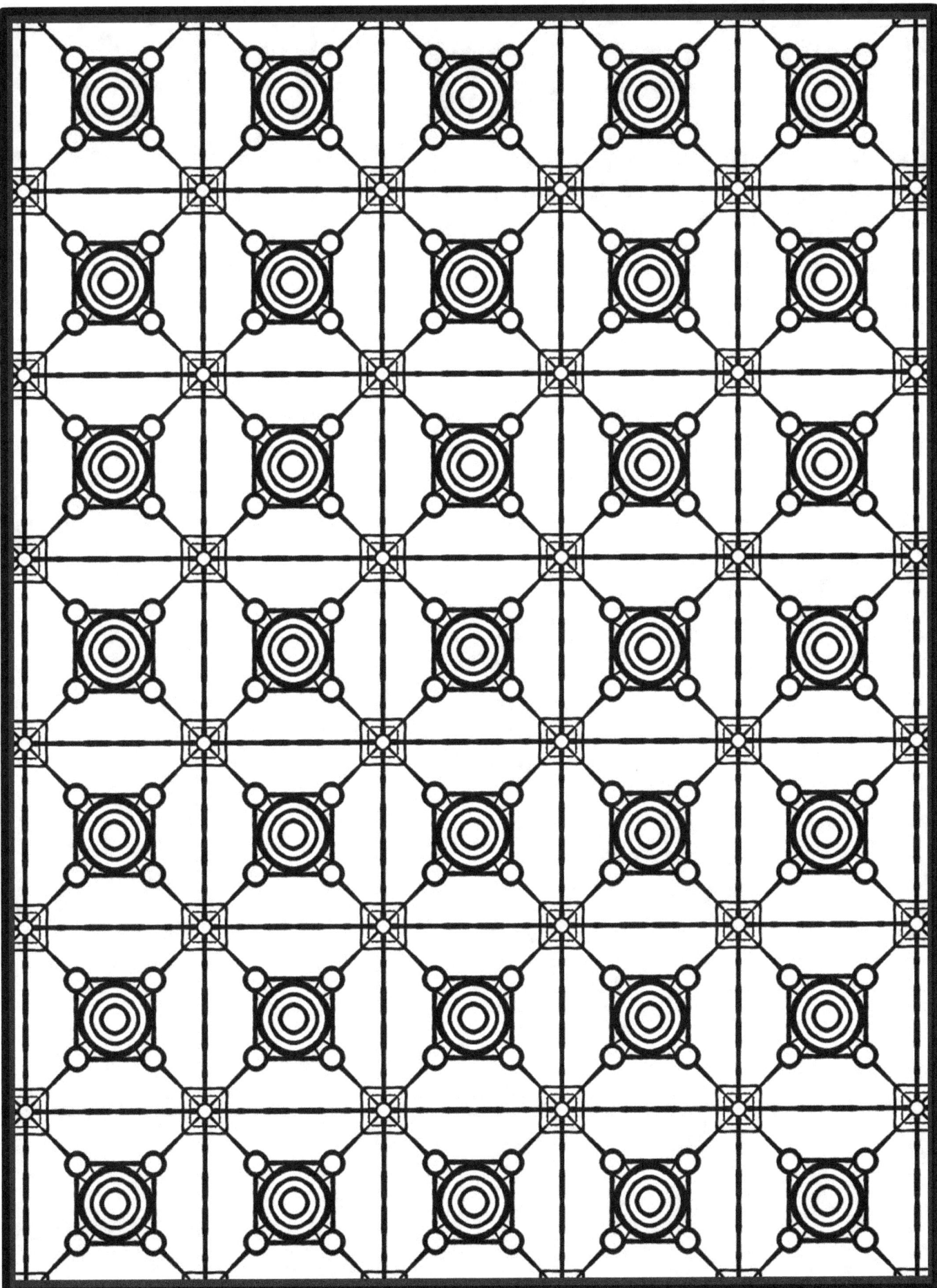

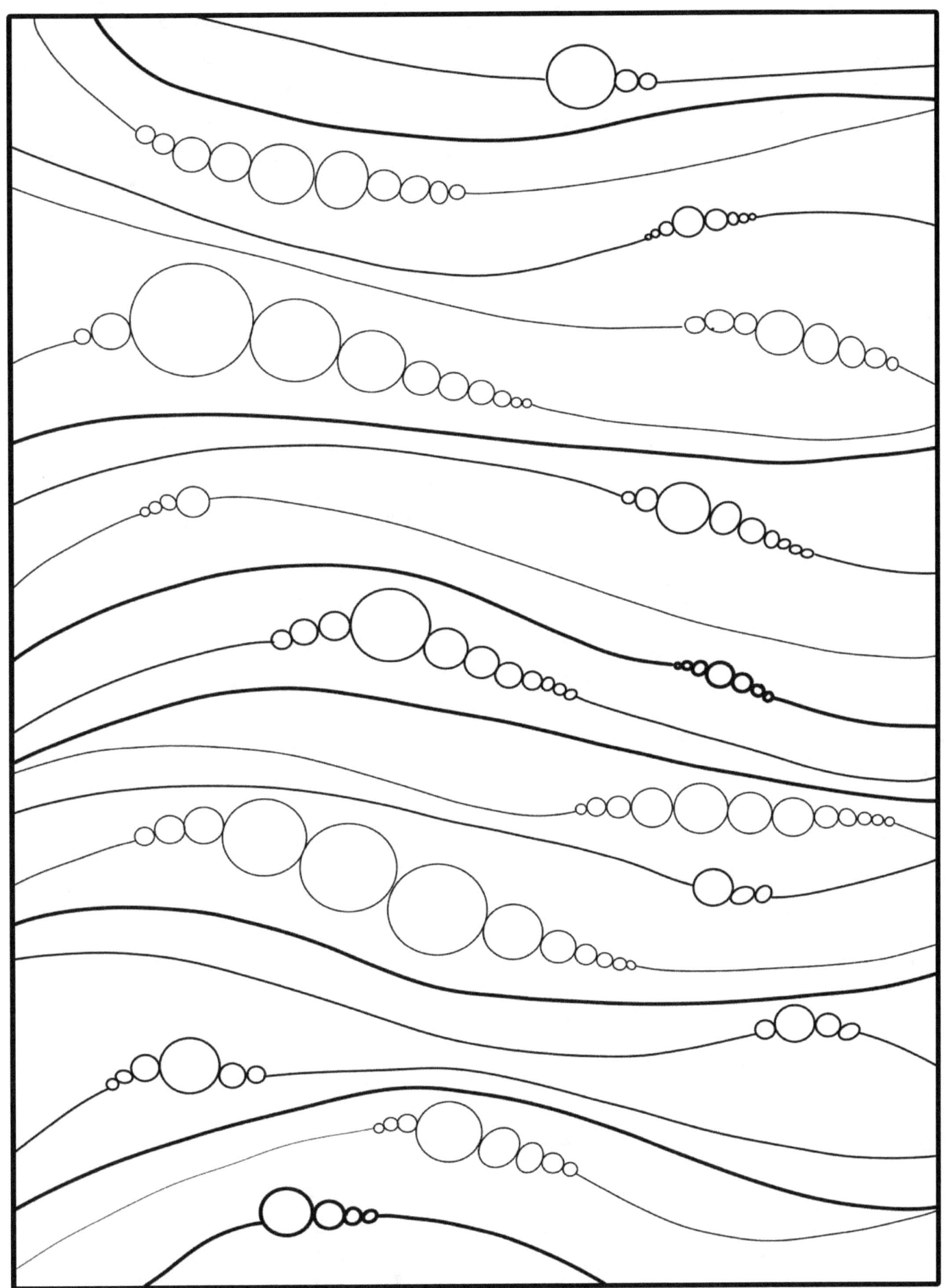

Color Test Page

Color Test Page

www.ingramcontent.com/pod-product-compliance
Lightning Source LLC
Chambersburg PA
CBHW080515220526
45465CB00006B/2496